Lights On!

Ike Hoover
Electrifies
the White House

By
Cynthia Simmelink Becker

Illustrated by
Benjamin Hummel

Filter Press, LLC • Palmer Lake, Colorado

ISBN: 978-0-86541-244-6

Library of Congress Cataloging-in-Publication Data

Names: Becker, Cynthia S. (Cynthia Simmelink), author. | Hummel, Benjamin,
    illustrator.
Title: Lights on! : Ike Hoover electrifies the White House / Cynthia
    Simmelink Becker ; illustrated by Benjamin Hummel.
Description: Palmer Lake, Colorado : Filter Press, LLC, 2017. | Audience: K
    to Grade 3.
Identifiers: LCCN 2017019335 | ISBN 9780865412446 (hardcover : alk. paper)
Subjects: LCSH: Hoover, Irwin Hood, 1871-1933. | White House (Washington,
    D.C.)--History--19th century--Juvenile literature. |
    Electrification--Washington (D.C.)--History--19th century--Juvenile
    literature. | White House (Washington,
    D.C.)--Employees--Biography--Juvenile literature. | Edison General
    Electric Company--Employees--Biography--Juvenile literature.
Classification: LCC F204.W5 B43 2017 | DDC 975.3--dc23 LC record available
at https://lccn.loc.gov/2017019335

Published by Filter Press, LLC, Palmer Lake, Colorado
info@FilterPressBooks.com / 888.570.2663

Printed in South Korea

*In loving memory of
Cynthia Becker,
fellow writer and friend.
To see this book come to life
after Cynthia left this earth
fills us with great sadness.
But we will read Lights On!
with many fond memories.
Cynthia enlightened us about this unique period
in history and our country's early scientific advances.
We will miss her curiosity, her dedication to facts,
her ability to find wonderful stories to tell,
and her good humor.
Above all, we are grateful for the precious time
she was with us. We will miss her always.*

*~ Cynthia's SCBWI Writing Critique Group:
Nancy Bentley, Cara Davies, Maria Faulconer,
Dian Curtis Regan, Carol Reinsma, Jill Woods.*

Washington City, District of Columbia

One crisp spring morning in 1891, a skinny young man with a long nose walked up the driveway to the President's House. He wore freshly washed work clothes and carried a wooden toolbox. He entered the basement by the servants' door in the rear.

"Irwin Hoover reporting for work," he said to the first man he saw. "Mr. Edison sent me."

The man frowned. "Look mighty young for such a big job. How old are you?"

"Nineteen, sir." Irwin stood as straight and tall as possible. "I was trained in the Edison General Electric Company shop. Learned all about wiring for electric lights. Mr. Edison's lights are a wonder. They're going to replace candles and kerosene lamps. Gas lights, too."

"So I've heard," the man said. He shook hands with Irwin. "Name's Samuel. I'll take you to see Admiral Baird. He's the Navy man in charge of this electrification project."

Samuel turned toward a dark hallway. "Come along, Ike."

"Pardon, sir. My name is Irwin."

Samuel paid no attention. He introduced "Ike the Electrician" to the cook, the washerwoman, and the gardener. From that day on, Irwin became "Ike" to everyone in the President's House.

They found the admiral in the large State, War, and Navy Building next door. The admiral was inspecting the new generator that would supply electric power to both buildings.

"My men started wiring and hanging new lights," the admiral told Ike. "But nothing worked properly. So, I asked Mr. Edison to send over his best electrician."

Ike's mouth stretched into a wide grin.

Admiral Baird looked Ike up and down, then asked the same question that Samuel had asked. "How old are you?"

"Nineteen, sir," Ike said. "I learned all about wiring electric lights in Mr. Edison's shop."

"Well, I trust Mr. Edison," the admiral said. "Check all the work my men did. Fix their mistakes. Then finish wiring the main floor. After that, wire the upper floors. Samuel will be your helper."

Without another word, he turned back to the generator.

"Come along," said Samuel. "We'll go back to the President's House, and I'll show you around."

As they walked, Samuel gave Ike tips about working in the great mansion.

"President and Mrs. Harrison keep a strict schedule. Breakfast at 8:30, lunch at 1:30, dinner at 6:30. Be careful you don't disturb them."

They returned to the basement. Then Samuel led the way up the stairs. Ike stopped on the top step and looked around. He had never seen such a house. The center hallway was long. The ceilings were high. The wooden floors were so polished he could see his reflection.

Ike looked into a large formal dining room. The polished table shone like a pool of water in the morning light. He counted thirty-two chairs around the table. Two very large glass chandeliers hung from the ceiling. Ike wondered if they had been wired for electricity.

"The President's family takes their meals in this smaller room," Samuel said, pointing to the left.

The family dining room looked large to Ike. He ate breakfast and supper every day in his parents' small kitchen.

Farther along the main hallway, bright red and blue patterns shimmered on the wooden floor. Morning sunlight filtered through a wall of colored glass. Samuel told Ike that a famous New York City artist created the glass wall. His name was Louis Comfort Tiffany.

A glass door in the wall opened to an entrance hall. "This is where guests arrive," Samuel said.

Across the main hallway, three elegant reception rooms stood open. One was painted and furnished in green. The middle room's curved walls were blue. Ike had never seen a room with no corners. The third room had red walls. Its ceiling was painted with red, white, and blue ribbons and silver, gold, and copper stars.

At the far end of the hall, Ike could see the wide ballroom called the East Room. Ike looked from one end of the room to the other. *My family's whole house would fit inside here*, he thought.

Samuel led the way up another set of stairs. "President Harrison and his staff have offices at this end of the second floor. The President works at his desk from nine in the morning 'til noon. Don't disturb him," Samuel warned.

They stepped through a door into the family quarters.

The head housekeeper appeared quickly. She was eager to tell Ike about the family. She spoke almost in a whisper. "There's more than just the President and his missus living here. Their daughter, Mary, and her husband have the northwest corner bedroom. The dressing room beside it is the nursery for their daughter, Mary, and their little boy, Benjamin. He has a German nurse to look after him.

"The Harrison's son, Russell, and his wife, Mary, are often here," the housekeeper continued. "They have a little daughter, Marthena.

"Then there is a niece, Mary Dimmick. Just think. Four Marys in the house. Don't you know that can get confusing!"

"Mrs. Harrison's father lives here, too. Reverend Scott is a kind old gentleman. Nearly ninety he is."

The housekeeper led the way past the President's bedroom. She opened a door and motioned for Ike to look inside.

"It's a toilet! The only one in the house," she said proudly.

What a luxury, Ike thought. His family did not have such a convenience. Like all the neighbors, his family had an outdoor privy. Ike had spotted privies for the staff behind the President's House.

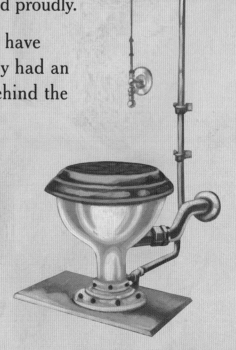

Samuel pointed out a ladder at the end of the hall. It stretched upward through a hole in the ceiling. "That is how you get to the third floor. Mostly storage up there."

Ike eyed the small opening. Carrying tools and supplies and rolls of wire up that ladder would be a challenge.

Ike had another worry. Patterned paper and painted designs decorated the walls and ceilings throughout the house. He would need to be ever so careful as he cut holes for electric wires.

After his tour, Ike got right to work inspecting the wiring done by the admiral's men. He showed Samuel how to make the simple repairs. Ike tackled the problems that needed complete rewiring.

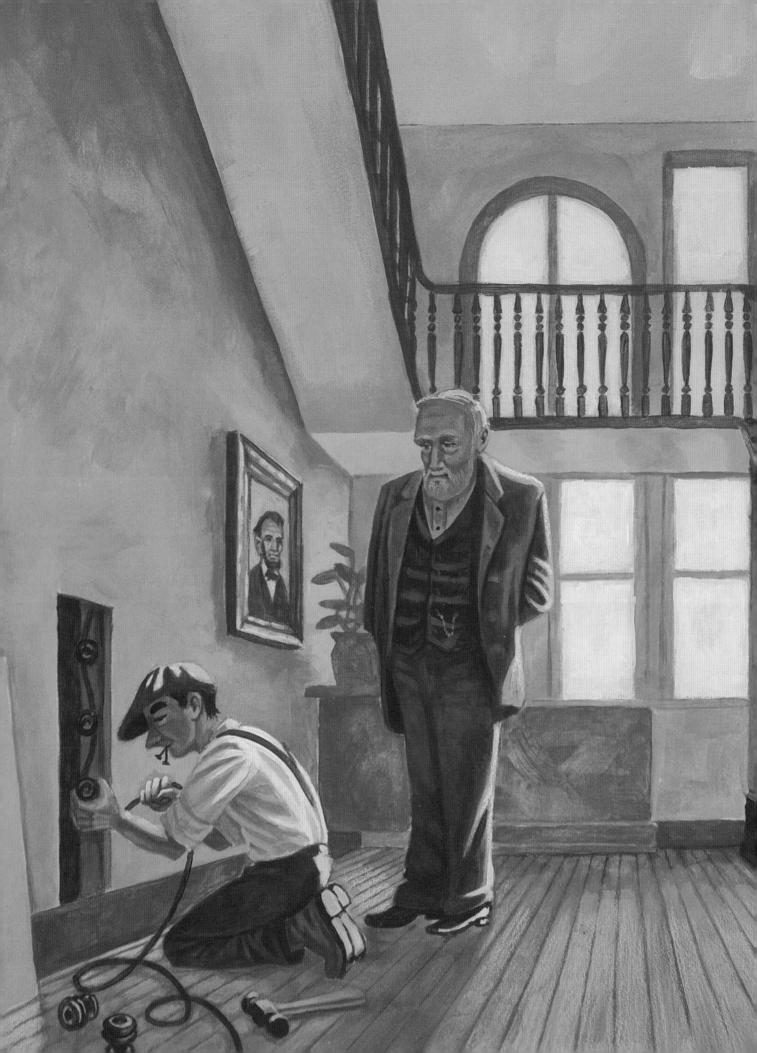

The following day, Ike was on his knees drilling a hole. He heard a voice behind him. "If those wires touch the wall, will the house catch on fire?"

Ike answered without looking up. "The wire is coated with tin and covered in rubber, then wrapped in waterproof cotton. We use ceramic knobs and tubes to hold the wire in place. Keeps it from rubbing against the wall." Ike slipped a piece of leather under the head of a nail and hammered a knob to a wooden beam in the wall.

"Most interesting," said the voice. "You must be Ike the Electrician."

Ike turned his head. A plump man with white hair and a neatly trimmed beard stood behind him.

The man held out his hand. "We are so pleased to have your services here."

"Mr. …Mr. President!" Ike stammered. He scrambled to stand up and shake the offered hand. "It's an honor to work in this house, sir."

Ike found many surprises in the President's House. A door at the west end opened into a large room with glass walls and a glass roof. This was the conservatory. It was filled with flowers and fruits trees. Real oranges and lemons grew fat on the branches. He saw several small greenhouses outside, all filled with plants. Orchids were Mrs. Harrison's favorite flower. They bloomed in pretty pots throughout the President's House.

Ike worked hard but found time to make friends with
the staff. His favorite was Dolly Johnson, the cook. She
worked in a basement kitchen that looked like a cave.
Two open fireplaces, each large enough to roast a
whole pig on a spit, took up most of the room.

Dolly prepared the simple foods
the Harrisons had enjoyed back home
in Indiana. Her kitchen was filled
with tempting smells. Chicken
with noodles. Pumpkin soup.

Onion pie. Bread and butter pickles. Persimmon pudding. Ike stopped every morning to sample a few of Dolly's buttermilk biscuits, hot from the oven and drizzled with sorghum.

In one basement room, Ike was surprised to find a leather-covered billiard table. A rack on the wall held the cue sticks neatly in place. Dolly told him the entire Harrison family, even the ladies, enjoyed the game. They spent many happy afternoons hidden away in the basement playing billiards.

At last, work on the main floor was finished. Ike and Samuel used the hydraulic elevator to carry tools and rolls of wire to the second floor. Next they lugged supplies up the ladder. Some boxes barely fit through the opening to the third floor.

Ike and Samuel used kerosene lamps to light the dark attic. Crawling across the ceiling beams, they unrolled wire. Ike cut holes and dangled wires into the second-floor rooms. Later he would connect the wires to ceiling lights.

One day Ike saw two tiny black eyes staring at him from behind his toolbox. With a scritch and scratch of claws on wood, the little animal scurried away. It was long and low to the ground with a furry tail. *Too big for a rat,* Ike thought.

Ike asked Samuel about the strange creature in the attic.

"A ferret!" Samuel rolled his eyes. "When the Harrisons moved in, this house was overrun with rats. Mrs. Harrison could not abide rats. She tried traps and poison. She hired men to shoot those pests. Nothing worked. Then she heard that ferrets eat rats. Mrs. Harrison bought a passel of those critters. I had to carry them to the attic and turn them loose. It worked. The ferrets slipped about in the shadows chasing rats. Now, we keep a couple in the basement, too."

Ike thought Mrs. Harrison was a smart woman.

At last, the work in the attic was finished. Ike began to install lights and switches on the second floor. Soon new eyes watched him. All the President's family wanted to know about the electrical equipment. Ike got used to having a Harrison or two peeking over his shoulder. They asked questions, and he tried his best to answer them.

Ike's own family was eager to hear about the President's family.

In the evenings, Ike told his family about his day. "Imagine me, barely out of knickers, explaining electric wiring to the President of the United States!"

His younger brother, James, wanted to hear every detail again.

"Early to bed and early to rise. That is the Harrison motto," he said. Ike did not want to gossip. However, once in a while he offered an observation. "The President is very careful about his appearance," Ike said at supper one night. "He brought his own barber all the way from Indiana. The President likes his hair and beard trimmed just so."

Ike described Mrs. Harrison as "homey, kind, and motherly." She was also an artist. She taught china painting classes for Washington ladies.

President and Mrs. Harrison enjoyed spending time with their family. They did not give many large dinner parties, but they often attended theater performances.

Every Wednesday afternoon the President took a long walk. He liked the time alone. In bad weather he rode in his dark green carriage, a Studebaker Landau. On those afternoons, Ike did his drilling and wiring in the President's office.

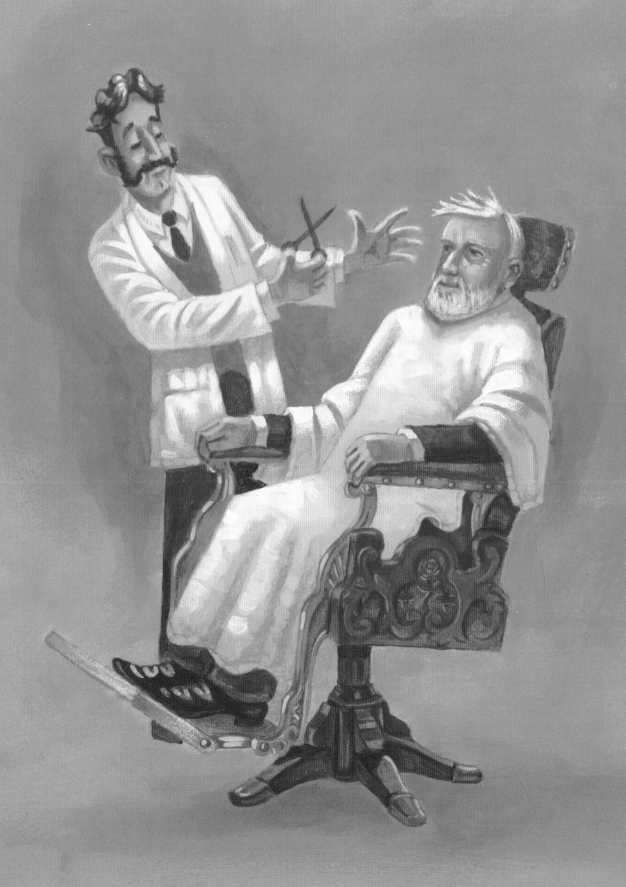

Ike replaced the metal candleholders on the walls throughout the house with electric lamps. He wired old gas chandeliers for electricity. Ike was making progress.

Mrs. Harrison was worried. "What will we do if the electric lights go out?"

The President was quick to solve the problem. "Leave a few of the old gas lights in working order," he told Ike.

The summer turned hot and damp. Ike's skin felt sticky, and his clothes were wet. Sweat rolled down his face. It dripped from his chin as he worked. Mosquitoes flew in through the open windows to pester everyone. Sewer gases filled the air with an awful smell.

The President and his family went to the seashore on vacation.

Ike kept working.

When the Harrisons returned at the end of summer, the work was done. More than 1,000 light bulbs were ready to brighten the mansion.

Ike toured every room one last time. He pushed the round buttons to be sure each light turned on and off. He knew all the nooks and crannies of the famous house. The staff was like family. He was sad to leave.

On his last workday, Ike walked slowly up the driveway. The big white house sat like a giant birthday cake on a green tablecloth. The American flag fluttered on the rooftop. President Harrison had the pole installed there. Ike remembered standing with the staff on July 4th, the day the new forty-four star flag flew for the first time. The forty-fourth star was for the new state of Wyoming.

Two days after he left, Ike received a letter from the President's House. It was an offer of a job to be the President's electrician.

The Harrisons were afraid to touch the new electric switches. They wanted Ike to turn the lights on at night and turn them off after they went to bed. Of course, he would repair any electrical problems, too.

The new job paid less than Ike earned from Mr. Edison, but he loved working in the President's House.

"I'll do it," Ike said.

A few weeks later, on September 24, 1891, President and Mrs. Harrison gave a dinner party. The Marine Band played while guests strolled among the ferns and flowers in the conservatory.

When it was time for dinner, the President led the guests down the hall to the East Room.

The great ballroom was dark.

Guests spoke in whispers as they entered.

When everyone was gathered, the President gave a signal.

Ike pushed the switch.

A burst of light brightened the room and glowed on the faces of the guests.

"Ahhh," everyone gasped.

Then they clapped and cheered.

Ike nearly burst with pride.

He had electrified the President's House.

Ike Hoover

Irwin "Ike" Hoover was born in Washington, District of Columbia, on October 24, 1871. He had two jobs in his life. He went to work for the Edison Electric Company around 1889. In September 1891, he began a 42-year career in the President's House. He started as the house electrician. In the 1910 census, Ike listed his job as "Doorkeeper at the Executive Mansion." In 1920 he was "Clerk at the White House." By 1930 he called his occupation "Executive with the U.S. Government."

The White House Historical Association reports Ike held the title of Chief Usher from 1913 to 1933. He was the official guardian at the front door and decided who was allowed into the White House. Ike supervised a large staff and coordinated official dinners, receptions, and ceremonies, including Alice Roosevelt's wedding.

Ike made lasting friendships with children of the various presidents he served, as this May 13, 1929, TIME Magazine story shows:

…to the White House last week went a…young man, well-dressed and with a manner. His wife and two children were with him.

"I wish to see Mr. Hoover," he said politely to the guard.

"Have you an appointment?"

"Yes, I telephoned Mr. Hoover."

The guard went away, then returned and said: "I'm sorry but the President isn't in."

"Oh," explained the well-mannered young man, "I don't want to see President Hoover, but Ike Hoover."

Head Usher Irwin Hood Hoover of the White House warmly greeted the young man whom he well remembered as Archie Roosevelt [son of Theodore Roosevelt].

On September 14, 1933, Ike Hoover left work as usual and died of a heart attack that evening. President Franklin D. Roosevelt announced Ike's death.

It was Ike who met me at the door when I came to make the White House my home…[H]is passing is a tremendous personal loss…the Nation, too, has lost a true friend and faithful public servant who, during every Administration since that of President Harrison, has given his best to his government.

Benjamin Harrison

Benjamin Harrison (1833-1901) was the 23rd President of the United States. He was also the grandson of the 21st president, William Henry Harrison. During the Civil War, Benjamin Harrison served as a Colonel in the Volunteer Infantry. He practiced law in Indiana before being elected to the United States Senate (1881-1887). Known for common sense and firm decisions, he served one term as U.S. President (1889-1893).

Thomas Edison

Thomas Alva Edison (1847-1931) filed his first patent application for Improvement in Electric Lights (U.S. Patent 0,214,636) on October 14, 1878. His first carbon filament light bulb burned for 13.5 hours. More than a year later, he developed a carbonized bamboo filament that burned over 1,200 hours. The light bulb became one of the first widely available applications of electrical power.

Author's Notes

Unitl 1901 the Executive Mansion was the official name of the President's home. Many people called it the President's House. Theodore Roosevelt changed the name to The White House in 1901.

The huge State, War, and Navy Building is now the Eisenhower Executive Office Building. It sits next to the White House, facing 17th Street NW. In 1891, Congress provided $13,450 to electrify this building and the President's House. The generating plant for both buildings was in the basement of the State, War and Navy Building. A cable strung across the yard and through a conservatory window carried electricity to the President's House.

The Edison General Electric Company sent two employees to make the electric conversion. Ike Hoover did not name the other man in his memoirs. It appears the second man worked primarily in the State, War and Navy Building. I chose to leave him out of the story. Samuel is a character of my creation to serve as Ike's helper.

In his memoir, Ike Hoover stated that sixteen employees worked in the President's House when he arrived. Dolly the cook was the only staff member identified by name. There were "not more than half a dozen domestic help"—the cook, housekeepers, and laundry workers. The Executive Office staff was limited to ten people including "four doorkeepers and messengers."

Wyoming became a state on July 10, 1890, but its new flag did not fly over the President's House until the following July 4th. Starting in 1819, a new flag becomes official on the Fourth of July following the date of a state's admission.

The Tiffany doors were commissioned in 1882 by President Chester Arthur. They replaced clear glass in the front door and the interior screen. The Tiffany glass was permanently removed in 1902 during White House remodeling.

If the Harrisons had been afraid to switch the lights on and off in the White House, it was a fear they quickly overcame. President Harrison had his home wired for electricity soon after he left office and returned to Indianapolis. His son-in-law, James Robert McKee, became a vice-president at General Electric and worked for GE until 1913.

The Census Bureau reports that electricity represented only 0.3 percent of all power used in the United States in 1890. The majority of power (76.9 percent) came from steam. Within fifteen years (1905), electricity represented 10.9 percent of power usage. In 1892, customers paid around $5 per kilowatt-hour for electricity. In 2010, the comparable price was nine cents.

Glossary

Billiard table – similar to a pool table. A player uses a special stick, called a cue, to knock balls into holes at the corners and sides of the table.

Chandelier – a light fixture that hangs from the ceiling and has many pieces of glass hanging from it to reflect light.

Convenience – an old-fashioned polite term for a toilet.

Electrician – a person who installs and repairs the wiring that carries electricity.

Electricity – a type of power caused by the motion of electrons and protons.

Electrify – to prepare a building to use electricity.

Generator – a machine that produces electricity by turning a magnet inside a coil of wire.

Kerosene – a thin, colorless oil used to fuel lamps and heat homes.

Knickers – knee-length pants worn by boys.

Persimmon – a red-orange fruit shaped like a plum that is sweet tasting when soft and ripe.

Sewer gases –foul smelling vapors produced by decaying waste in sewer pipes.

Sorghum – a sweet syrup made from sorghum plants.

Spit – a long pointed rod that holds meat over a fire for cooking.

Studebaker Landau – a type of horse-drawn carriage with a roof that could be lowered or removed in good weather. The Studebaker company later built automobiles.

Resources

Dini, David A. *Some History of Residential Wiring Practices in the U.S.* Underwriters Laboratories, Inc. 2006. Abstract at: (https://www.dli.mn.gov/ccld/PDF/eli_GFCI_history.pdf)

Froncek, Thomas, Editor. *The City of Washington, An Illustrated History.* New York: Alfred A. Knopf, 1977.

Hoover, Irwin Hood. *My 42 Years in the White House.* New York: Houghton Mifflin, 1934.

Sievers, Henry J. *Benjamin Harrison.* Chicago: Henry Regnery Company, 1952.

Thomas Alva Edison and his inventions (http://edison.rutgers.edu/list.htm)

Time Magazine, March 4, 1929.

Washington Post, September 24, 1891.

Whitcomb, John and Claire. *Real Life in the White House.* New York: Rutledge, 2000.

The White House Historical Association (www.whitehousehistory.org)

The White House Museum (www.whitehousemuseum.org)

About the Author

Cynthia Simmelink Becker was passionate about history, especially when it came to writing biographies of those often overlooked by history. Among the books she wrote, two were about Chipeta, an influential Southern Ute woman. Ike Hoover's untold story also lent itself well to Cynthia's interests and her research and storytelling skills.

Cynthia made her home in Pueblo, Colorado, with her husband, David. She passed away in 2016, leaving Lights On! in the care of her husband, her writers' group, and Filter Press.

About the Illustrator

Benjamin Hummel has always been a student of history, and his illustrations are characterized by a joyful sense of nostalgia and of a time gone by. His light-hearted illustrations have appeared in numerous books, magazines, and greeting cards. When he is not illustrating children's books, or creating 3D chalk art paintings at festivals, he teaches illustration at Rocky Mountain College of Art and Design.

Benjamin conducts his life while managing a debilitating autoimmune disease. This disease resulted in two liver transplants. As a result of his renewed lease on life, Benjamin dedicates his work to the joy of living. He paints to overcome the struggles of everyday life and to encourage others to live life more fully.